THE HIP-HOP REVOLUTION

LIL BUCK
INSPIRING CHANGE THROUGH DANCE

KATE MIKOLEY

Enslow Publishing
101 W. 23rd Street
Suite 240
New York, NY 10011
USA

enslow.com

Published in 2020 by Enslow Publishing, LLC.
101 W. 23rd Street, Suite 240, New York, NY 10011

Cataloging-in-Publication Data

Names: Mikoley, Kate.
Title: Lil Buck: inspiring change through dance / Kate Mikoley.
Description: New York : Enslow Publishing, 2020. | Series: The hip-hop revolution |
Audience: Grade 5 | Includes bibliographical references and index.
Identifiers: ISBN 9781978509689 (library bound) | ISBN 9781978510357 (pbk.) |
ISBN 9781978510371 (6 pack)
Subjects: LCSH: Lil Buck, 1988—Juvenile literature. | Dancers—United States—
Biography—Juvenile literature.
Classification: LCC GV1785.L553 M63 2020 | DDC 792.8028092 [B]—dc23

Printed in the United States of America

To Our Readers: We have done our best to make sure all websites in this book were active and appropriate when we went to press. However, the author and the publisher have no control over and assume no liability for the material available on those websites or on any websites they may link to. Any comments or suggestions can be sent by email to customerservice@enslow.com.

CONTENTS

JOOKIN IN MEMPHIS

For many people, dancing is a fun way to express themselves. For Lil Buck, it's about more than just himself. He thinks dance can bring people together. Maybe it can even make the world a better place. He even started a group to help inspire others and show dance as an important art form.

Lil Buck was born in Chicago, Illinois, on May 25, 1988. His real name is Charles Riley. As a child, he moved to Memphis, Tennessee, with his family. Lil Buck started dancing when he was six. By the time he was about twelve, he was jookin!

JOOKIN DOWN THE STREET

Jookin started in Memphis, where Lil Buck grew up. It's a kind of street dance. Jookin grew from another kind

In 2018, Lil Buck attended the opening for the movie *The Nutcracker and the Four Realms*. In the film, he provided the movements for the Mouse King.

of dance popular in Memphis called the gangsta walk. This is a type of line dance that involves looking really confident. Lil Buck says he learned about jookin from his older sister. She learned about it at school. She was the first person to show him what it was.

After seeing his sister jookin, Lil Buck started getting into it, too. He began dancing in groups around Memphis. The first time he saw what he considered to be true jookin was at a skating rink called the Crystal Palace. There he saw a dancer who really inspired him.

GETTING BETTER WITH BALLET

At seventeen, Lil Buck was practicing with a group when a ballet teacher spotted him. The teacher was impressed with how well he could spin on his toes. She invited him to study with the New Ballet Ensemble and School in Memphis. Already a skilled dancer, but new to ballet, Lil Buck was worried about having to wear tights. When he was told he wouldn't have to, he took the offer. He did ballet for more than three years. He saw how flexible the other dancers were. He wanted to be that flexible, too. This gave him a goal.

History of Jookin

Jookin began in Memphis around the 1980s. Some call it other names, such as bucking or urban ballet. Jookin grew from the underground rap music that was being made in Memphis. It began as a simple one-two step. It now includes popping, slides, glides, toe spins, and waves.

Lil Buck's ability to dance on his toes is one of the things that sets him apart from many other dancers.

Some of Lil Buck's dance moves, such as this one, can appear almost impossible. These kinds of moves are part of his unique style.

Ballet gave Lil Buck the chance to improve his own dance skills. He likes to tell people about how he did ballet so others, especially boys, aren't afraid of taking a ballet class. "You can still be you and take ballet," he told the *New York Times*.[1] He says it can help people learn skills such as balance and control. These are key to all kinds of dance.

"You can still be you and take ballet."

FINDING HIS GROOVE

Jookin is based in freestyle dancing. This means there aren't really any strict rules. The dancer can come up with their own moves. Lil Buck was able to combine what he learned from ballet with jookin. He formed his own unique style.

Finding his style took lots of practice. When Lil Buck was in high school, he decided he wanted to be able to stay up on his toes longer than anyone else! He'd walk around his house on his toes all day. This way, he could build the strength needed to dance on his toes. It also helped him get used to how it felt.

Lil Buck and his personal dance style became well known around Memphis. He was in dance videos that were put on YouTube, as well as a few DVDs on jookin that were made in Memphis.

MOVING ON UP

The way Lil Buck's feet move sets him apart from other dancers. He can bend and move his feet in ways other people can't. For the most part, his skills are due to a lot of hard work and practice. However, sometimes good things can also happen by accident.

A NATURAL GIFT

When he was in fourth grade, Lil Buck hurt his ankle. It snapped. Years later, when he was eighteen, he hurt it again. A few months after that, he was doing some stretches when his ankle popped. All these things seem like they could have ruined his future in

"I'm really flexible on some spots naturally, but I do work at it."

Lil Buck's flexibility takes center stage during a performance at an Apple store in San Francisco, California, in 2017.

dance. In Lil Buck's case, they helped. The day after the stretching accident, his ankles felt loose and easy to move. Lil Buck has called his flexibility a gift. But he doesn't take it for granted.

"I'm really flexible on some spots naturally, but I do work at it," he said at a National YoungArts Foundation event.[1] He also said he does stretches and exercises to keep his ankles strong.

Because of his hard work and talent, it wasn't long before others, even outside of Memphis, saw how great Lil Buck was.

Shown here doing a handstand in 2011, Lil Buck has become famous not only for dancing, but also for choreographing.

LIL BUCK'S BIG BREAK

At nineteen, Lil Buck went to Los Angeles, California. Someone had contacted him through MySpace, an early social media site. This person wanted him to dance in a music video for a local artist. Lil Buck flew out there with a friend who also jooked. Lil Buck then got a job in a commercial. He also thought he could become a backup dancer for hip-hop artists. At the time, he probably didn't know he'd end up being famous for much more than being a backup dancer.

Soon, singer and songwriter Janelle Monáe saw one of Lil Buck's videos on YouTube. She wanted him to dance in one of her music videos. The video was for Monáe's hit song "Tightrope." The song was nominated for a Grammy Award. The video, which Lil Buck both danced in and helped choreograph, was nominated for Best Choreography at the MTV Video Music Awards in 2010. Although the video lost to Lady Gaga's "Bad Romance," it helped Lil Buck and the entire Memphis jookin community gain attention. The video featured Monáe, Lil Buck, and many others performing some of the fancy moves jookin is known for.

Lil Buck now had the attention of many people. Soon, he would be known by many more.

THE JOOKIN SWAN

A turning point in Lil Buck's career happened when he danced alongside another artist named Yo-Yo Ma. A famous cello player, Yo-Yo Ma's main style of music is classical. This music is often thought of as very sophisticated. Yo-Yo Ma is also known for working with artists from many styles and cultures.

A former dancer with the New York City Ballet named Damian Woetzel saw Lil Buck dance. He was impressed. He was so impressed that in 2011, he brought Lil Buck and Yo-Yo Ma together to perform.

Going Viral

"Going viral" means someone or something spreads quickly, usually on the internet, and becomes popular. While Lil Buck was performing with Yo-Yo Ma, a famous director named Spike Jonze was watching. Jonze filmed the piece on his phone and posted it on the internet. Soon, people around the world saw Lil Buck.

Lil Buck took the stage with Yo-Yo Ma (*bottom left corner*) again in June 2011 to perform in Central Park in New York City.

Yo-Yo Ma played a piece on his cello called "The Swan." At the same time, Lil Buck danced his own version of a classic ballet dance called *The Dying Swan*. Of course, his dance was quite unique and displayed Lil Buck's distinct style. The crowd was impressed with how well the two artists' styles came together.

WORLDWIDE SUCCESS

After the video went viral, Lil Buck and Yo-Yo Ma kept working together. In late 2011, they went to China for an event meant to show the art and culture of both the United States and China. The US–China Forum on the Arts and Culture included actors, authors, and many others. People talked about movies and writing, showcased many kinds of music, and even discussed food.

This was Lil Buck's first trip out of the United States. He and Yo-Yo Ma performed their piece once again. While in China, Lil

"For me to perform to classical with Yo-Yo just showed the world what we already knew was possible."[1]

Buck danced all around the city of Beijing. He even danced on the Great Wall of China!

PERFORMING WITH THE QUEEN OF POP

Lil Buck's fame was now growing even more. People who had never heard of jookin before were becoming fans of him. One big fan was Madonna. She's a pop singer who became famous in the 1980s. She is still well known today and often referred to as the "Queen of Pop." In 2012, she was set to perform in the Super Bowl halftime show.

Madonna is known for using many showy dance moves onstage. So when people heard she was doing the halftime show, they expected something crazy. But the show wasn't just her. It included many other artists and dancers. Lil Buck was one of them! Many times, the dancers on stage with an artist are just there to be in the background. They can be used to make the star look good. In this case, some say Lil Buck was a highlight of the show.

Since the Super Bowl performance, Lil Buck has continued to dance with Madonna. He went on tour with her in 2012. He also danced with her on her 2015–2016 Rebel Heart Tour.

Madonna's a big fan of Lil Buck. She even talked about him in a speech and spoke about his talent and drive.

DANCING FOR THE KING OF POP

In 2012, *Dance Magazine* included Lil Buck on its "25 to Watch" list. The article noted Lil Buck's "flowing moves."[2]

A Flashy Event

The Super Bowl halftime show is often one of the most exciting music and dance performances of the year. Some people only watch the game to see the halftime show! People were impressed with Madonna's show in 2012. But not just with her—they loved Lil Buck's moves, too!

Lil Buck (*right*) is shown here with Madonna during the 2012 Super Bowl halftime show. Eye-catching costumes are often a big part of the show.

Shown here at a 2014 awards ceremony, Lil Buck's ability to contort, or bend, his body in amazing ways landed him a part in Cirque du Soleil's *Michael Jackson ONE*.

The magazine was right—Lil Buck was a dancer to keep an eye on. He had been doing great things for years. He wasn't about to stop any time soon.

In addition to his fancy footwork and smooth moves, Lil Buck is known for his ability to bend his body. He can do this in ways many other great dancers can't. This skill came in handy when he was cast in a Cirque du Soleil show. Starting in 2013, he danced in the company's show *Michael Jackson ONE*. It took place in Las Vegas, Nevada, and was based on the music of an artist known as the "King of Pop." During his life, Michael Jackson (1958–2009) was known for his popular songs and his signature dance moves.

The Cirque du Soleil show featured many great performers, but some say Lil Buck and his incredible moves nearly stole the show. Lil Buck danced regularly in the show for nine months. He also remained "on call" for a time afterward. This meant he could be called to come back if the show needed him.

HELPING OTHERS

L il Buck has danced all over the world. He's been in a commercial for the car company Lexus. He was also in an Apple commercial for AirPods and the iPhone7. He's modeled clothing, danced onstage with huge stars, and performed on talk shows. He's even danced in movies!

TV SHOW APPEARANCES

In 2014, Lil Buck was a guest judge on the popular TV show *So You Think You Can Dance*. He had previously danced on the show with Janelle Monáe when she performed the song "Tightrope."

Lil Buck has also continued to work with artists from other fields. This brings people from many walks of life together. In 2015, he first performed in a show called *What Moves You*. This show was a collaboration with

In 2015, Lil Buck teamed up with the fashion company Versace. He's shown here at an event in New York City showing off sneakers he helped design.

another cello player, Ashley Bathgate. He'd later go on to perform the show with yet another cello player named Mihai Marica. The show explored the bond between movement and music. It was also meant to test the limits of each artist's "instrument." In Lil Buck's case, his instrument was his body. But Lil Buck's dance career is about more than just performing. He uses his art to help other people, too.

DANCING FOR THE GREATER GOOD

In 2016, Lil Buck cofounded an organization called Movement Art Is (MAI) with another dancer named Jon Boogz. They each have different dance styles, but both agree dance can help people. They think it can make the world a better place.

Lil Buck and Boogz met in California and started dancing together. They wanted to do more than just put on a show for people. They wanted to focus on big issues, such as racism and the environment. That's where MAI came in. The nonprofit puts together dance videos, films, and live shows addressing these kinds of issues.

Another thing MAI does is show people different dance styles. For a long time, people outside of Memphis

More than Entertainment

According to the founders of MAI, dance isn't just for entertaining people. It can also teach people important lessons. Lil Buck and Boogz perform dances with strong messages, often about important social topics such as violence and race.

From left to right, Lil Buck, spoken word artist Robin Sanders, and Jon Boogz performed together at a fund-raising event in 2016.

didn't really know about jookin. But now, with the help of MAI and Lil Buck, people are seeing it. Other than just showing them a cool form of dance, this can also help people learn about different cultures.

In 2018, Lil Buck and Boogz made a show called *Love Heals All Wounds*. They've taken the show to stages across the country. In the show, they use their moves to bring up social issues in the United States and the

Lil Buck works hard to promote arts education. He's shown here performing for a group of elementary school students through a program called Inner-City Arts.

world. Among them is climate change. Climate change refers to big and often harmful changes in the world's temperature, as well as other changes in weather.

Lil Buck has said that in addition to simply bringing up these issues, he wants the show to help people see that there are solutions. The answer is in the name of the show itself. The solution, Lil Buck says, is love.

Lil Buck proves that it's possible to use something you love to make a difference. In the dance world, he's made people see that ballet and hip-hop don't have to be two completely separate things. Lil Buck has taken jookin from the streets of Memphis to the world stage. He has also used dance to make people think about big problems that affect everyone. By thinking and talking about important issues, changes can happen.

"We want to focus on 'these things are out there'– but also on 'what is the solution?' There is a solution and a way out of this: love."[1]

TIMELINE

1988 Lil Buck is born May 25 in Chicago.

c. 2000 Lil Buck, now living in Memphis, starts learning about jookin.

2005 Lil Buck starts studying ballet.

2010 Lil Buck dances in Janelle Monáe's video for her song "Tightrope."

2011 Lil Buck's version of the dance *The Dying Swan*, with Yo-Yo Ma playing cello, is posted online and goes viral.

2011 Lil Buck goes to China for the US–China Forum on the Arts and Culture.

2012 *Dance Magazine* names Lil Buck on its "25 to Watch" list.

2012 Lil Buck performs at the Super Bowl with Madonna on February 5 and later goes on tour with her.

2013 Lil Buck starts dancing in the Cirque du Soleil show *Michael Jackson ONE* in Las Vegas.

2014 Lil Buck is a guest judge on *So You Think You Can Dance*.

2016 Lil Buck and Jon Boogz cofound Movement Art Is.

2018 Lil Buck and Jon Boogz tour across the country with their show *Love Heals All Wounds*.

CHAPTER NOTES

CHAPTER 1. JOOKIN IN MEMPHIS

1. Marina Harss, "Lil Buck and Jon Boogz, Dancing to Improve the World," *New York Times,* April 10, 2018, https://www.nytimes.com/2018/04/10/arts/dance/lil-buck-and-jon-boogz-love-heals-all-wounds.html.

CHAPTER 2. MOVING ON UP

1. Fernando González, "Lil' Buck and the Art of Jookin," Knight Foundation, January 23, 2015, https://knightfoundation.org/articles/lil-buck-and-art-jookin.

CHAPTER 3. WORLDWIDE SUCCESS

1. Evan Osnos, "Jookin on the Great Wall: Q. & A. with Lil Buck," *New Yorker,* February 26, 2013, https://www.newyorker.com/news/evan-osnos/jookin-on-the-great-wall-q-a-with-lil-buck.

2. "25 to Watch," *Dance Magazine,* December 16, 2011, https://www.dancemagazine.com/2012-25-to-watch-2306890106.html.

CHAPTER 4. HELPING OTHERS

1. Marina Harss, "Lil Buck and Jon Boogz, Dancing to Improve the World," *New York Times,* April 10, 2018, https://www.nytimes.com/2018/04/10/arts/dance/lil-buck-and-jon-boogz-love-heals-all-wounds.html.

GLOSSARY

choreograph To put together steps and create a dance to be performed.

Cirque du Soleil A Canadian theater company that puts on shows all over the world with different themes that feature elaborate sets, dances, and acrobatics.

collaboration A project done by two or more people.

confident Feeling that you are good at something.

culture The way of life, including beliefs, customs, and art, of a certain group of people.

flexible Able to bend one's body in ways that may be difficult for other people.

freestyle Made up on the spot; not having any strict rules.

organization A group formed for a certain purpose.

popping A kind of dance with quick, jerky moves.

racism Poor and unjust treatment of people because of their race.

sophisticated High culture, or very complex and developed.

unique Different in a way often thought to be good or special.

urban Having to do with large cities.

FURTHER READING

BOOKS

DeAngelis, Audrey, and Gina DeAngelis. *Hip-Hop Dance*. Minneapolis, MN: Essential Library, 2018.

Jones, Jen. *Top Dance Tips*. North Mankato, MN: Raintree, 2017.

Kjelle, Marylou Morano. *Trends in Hip-Hop Dance*. Hockessin, DE: Mitchell Lane Publishers, 2015.

Lanier, Wendy Hinote. *Hip-Hop Dance*. Lake Elmo, MN: Focus Readers, 2018.

WEBSITES

LILBUCK.COM
www.lilbuck.com
Check out a video of Lil Buck dancing, as well as links to his social media pages.

Memphis Jookin
www.memphisjookin.com/history/
Dive deeper into the history of Memphis jookin.

Movement Art Is
movementartis.com
Learn more about Lil Buck's organization Movement Art Is, which uses movement to inspire change.

INDEX